HOLLYWOOD
TRAINS

EDITED BY J. C. SUARÈS
TEXT BY J. SPENCER BECK

THOMASSON-GRANT

Published by Thomasson-Grant, Inc.

Copyright © 1994 J. C. Suarès.
Captions copyright © 1994 J. Spencer Beck.

Printed in Hong Kong.

ISBN 1-56566-066-8

00 99 98 97 96 95 94 5 4 3 2 1

Inquiries should be directed to:
Thomasson-Grant, Inc.
One Morton Drive, Suite 500
Charlottesville, VA 22903-6806
(804) 977-1780

THE MAN WITHOUT A STAR, 1955

*The only thing banjo-playing cowboy Kirk Douglas hates
more than barbed wire in this edgy range-war actioner-cum-love story
is the steam-spewing train bringing in more encroaching cattlemen.
Featuring the usual round of trigger-happy gunslingers, land-grabbing
ranchers, and saucy saloon girls, the King Vidor-directed yarn was
remade for television in 1969 with Tony Franciosa in the lead.*

What's faster than a speeding bullet, stronger than a steel locomotive, and able to leap Alpine passes in a single bound? Hollywood trains, of course. From the first silent shorts at the turn of the century to the big-budget box-office bonanzas of today, moviemakers' love affair with the railway car has marked some of the best-loved motion pictures of all time.

Hollywood's transportation of choice for almost a century, these speeding locomotives, transcontinental luxury liners, and streamlined railroad cars have graced more pictures with their steam-spewing, engine-churning glory and old-fashioned romance than all of the big-screen's automobiles, steamships, and airplanes combined. Often real-life models or meticulously crafted facsimiles of the originals, a number of trains have outshined their star passengers and made Hollywood history in their own right.

Assembling a cast of thousands and retooling the original railway cars for his epic about the building of the first transcontinental railroad, director John Ford created a classic in 1924 with *The Iron Horse* and defined the Western genre for future filmmakers in the process. Cecil B. deMille topped him fifteen years later with *Union Pacific*, and John Frankenheimer made both the trains and the French railwaymen who ran them the stars of his 1964 WWII actioner, *The Train*, starring Burt Lancaster.

Featured less prominently in countless film formats ranging from silent one-reelers and "B" Westerns to period dramas and love stories (the trainside farewell kiss is almost a cinematic cliché), the train setting is perhaps best remembered in hundreds of action-packed spy thrillers and mysteries.

From Josef von Sternberg's seminal story of wartime intrigue, *Shanghai Express*, to celluloid crowdpleasers like *Night Train to Munich* and *Murder on the Orient Express*, terror-filled train rides have made passengers and audiences alike cower in their seats and think twice before buying another railway ticket on a luxury locomotive.

Alfred Hitchcock, the master of suspense, is also the master of the train-mystery thriller, and claustrophobic railroad cars figure prominently in some of the director's best-loved films, including *The Lady Vanishes*, *Spellbound*, *Strangers on a Train*, and *North by Northwest*. Although these classics depend more on story line than technical wizardry (a model was used for outside shots of the speeding train in *The Lady Vanishes*), they provide more frame-for-frame fun-filled terror than any number of lackluster imitations.

Not every Hollywood train ride ends in murder and mayhem, however. Just as many end in *mirth* and mayhem, and in comedy classics such as *My Little Chickadee*, *The Palm Beach Story*, and *Some Like It Hot*, the side-splitting humor is still on track today. There are even a few pictures that manage to induce screams of laughter and screams of horror at the same time (*Throw Momma From the Train* and *Silver Streak*), and at least one celebrated train scene that is sure to make you cry (*Anna Karenina*).

Why have trains fascinated moviemakers and moviegoers for so long? Maybe it's the speed, or the sheer physical power of the diesel-driven machines. Or maybe it's just a longing for a bygone era when railroads were a one-way ticket to adventure—and good old-fashioned romance.

Greta Garbo and Fredric March
ANNA KARENINA, 1935 (RIGHT)

*Never has a train figured so sadly on the silver screen.
When the two-timing Tolstoy heroine in this luminous remake
of the Garbo-John Gilbert silent, Love, finally realizes she has lost
everything (husband, child, <u>and</u> paramour), she throws herself in
front of a departing train. As its lights catch her face in that final
scene, Garbo's sublime agony is captured for eternity in one
of Hollywood's most celebrated close-ups.*

Audrey Hepburn and Fred Astaire
FUNNY FACE, 1957 (FOLLOWING PAGES)

*Hepburn's gamine-in-Givenchy appeal was perfect in this
glorious musical satire-cum-love story of a lowly bookstore clerk
transformed into a high-fashion model by an Avedon-like photographer
(Astaire). Already falling in unrequited love with him, Hepburn cries
real tears when Astaire asks her to pose tragically à la Anna Karenina
beside a departing train at the Gare du Nord during the film's
glamorous whirlwind fashion shoot around Paris.*

Kirk Douglas
LAST TRAIN FROM GUN HILL, 1959 (ABOVE)
Remarkably similar to the Glenn Ford vehicle 3:10 to Yuma, *made two years earlier, this brooding Western again tells the tale of a lone cowboy trying to get out of town and onto a train with a killer he wants to bring to justice. Although a posse of vengeful townsfolk would rather solve matters themselves, both films end with the heroes departing by train and the bad guys departing into eternity after the obligatory* High Noon-*style shoot-outs.*

Barbara Stanwyck and Robert Preston
UNION PACIFIC, 1939 (RIGHT)
Assembling the usual cast of thousands for the "greatest train story ever told," Cecil B. deMille picked the Union Pacific railroad on the flip of a coin (the Santa Fe lost out) and mounted his last black-and-white epic for Paramount Pictures. Researched with piles of old documents and featuring real vintage trains and headlining stars such as Stanwyck (the UP's postmistress—with a brogue!), Preston (a gambler and thief), and Joel McCrea (the company's chief engineer), this saga of the building of the first transcontinental railway featured everything from a stunning train wreck and Indian attacks to an unforgettable cavalry rescue via railroad flatcars.

Audrey Hepburn and Gary Cooper

LOVE IN THE AFTERNOON, 1957 (ABOVE)

*Forget the thirty-year age difference; Hepburn and Cooper share
some genuinely touching moments in this sparkling Billy Wilder-directed
tribute to his idol, Ernst Lubitsch. With Hepburn playing the
daughter of a French private eye (Maurice Chevalier) hired to spy on
American playboy Cooper (with whom Hepburn falls in love),
the picture's de rigueur farewell scene at a Paris train station
adds a note of pathos to this fast-moving farce.*

Millie Perkins and Elvis Presley

WILD IN THE COUNTRY, 1961 (RIGHT)

*Leaving for college to become a literary giant, hillbilly Presley
says a tearful trainside goodbye to one of his three love interests
(Hope Lange and Tuesday Weld are the others) in this far-fetched star
vehicle based on the Clifford Odets play. More of a curiosity piece for
die-hard Elvis fans, the serious-minded if miscast effort still managed
to slip in a few of the King's musical numbers and featured a
young Christina Crawford in a rare screen appearance.*

Merle Oberon and Paul Lukas

BERLIN EXPRESS, 1948 (ABOVE)

*Luckily for this muddled WWII spy thriller about a "good" German
(Lukas) who wants to reunite the Fatherland, the train in the title keeps the
plot moving at a swift pace. Filmed in semi-documentary style and featuring
actual footage of bombed-out Berlin, the picture also features some overpopped
Hollywood corn. The scenes of jet-set-glamorous Oberon (a lowly German
government aide!) stumbling through the rubble of war in a series
of stunning Orry-Kelly gowns is Tinseltown at its tackiest.*

Barbara Stanwyck and Fred MacMurray

DOUBLE INDEMNITY, 1944 (RIGHT)

*This much-imitated but never-matched film-noir masterpiece
features one of Hollywood's most celebrated train scenes. Enticed by a rider
on her husband's insurance policy that allows her to collect double the face
value if he is killed by a moving train, blonde-bombshell Stanwyck finally
seduces mild-mannered MacMurray to hop aboard and help her commit
the crime. The dastardly deed done, MacMurray comes to the end of
his own line after being duped by his double-crossing accomplice.*

Eva Marie Saint and Cary Grant

NORTH BY NORTHWEST, 1959

*Although the character Grant plays in this classic Alfred Hitchcock
tale of mistaken indentity is best remembered being chased by a
crop-dusting plane, he earlier eludes the police dressed as a porter
on a speeding train. The exciting mystery/thriller/comedy, the
director's first collaboration with MGM, includes references to
many of Hitchcock's previous pictures, including his most
riveting railway romp,* Strangers on a Train.

Burt Lancaster and Wolfgang Preiss

THE TRAIN, 1965 (ABOVE)

Stunningly shot on location in France by director John Frankenheimer,
the chessboard-like montage of trains, tracks, and shunting yards is an inspired
setting for the game of wits between a Nazi colonel (Paul Scofield) trying to escape
France with a cache of priceless paintings and a railway engineer (Lancaster) tapped
by the French Resistance to stop him. Capturing the massive, real-life trains from
every angle possible by using a number of cameras simultaneously, the Oscar-
nominated film includes peerless action sequences that have helped make
it an all-time favorite among train enthusiasts everywhere.

Frank Sinatra

VON RYAN'S EXPRESS, 1965 (RIGHT)

Perfectly cast as a tough American colonel downed in a plane crash in
WWII Italy, the former bobby-sox idol-turned-mega-movie star shines in this
old-fashioned action-packed thriller. Commandeering a train in a desperate attempt
to flee with a group of American and British POWs to neutral Switzerland,
Sinatra and crew elude attacking Messerschmitts and the dumbest Nazis
this side of the Alps before the film's cliff-hanging (literally!) finale,
one of the most thrilling in train-movie history.

18

David Niven, Shirley MacLaine, and Cantinflas

AROUND THE WORLD IN EIGHTY DAYS, 1956

*Although showman Mike Todd's Jules Verne-inspired
wide-screen spectacle won five Oscars including Best Picture,
many critics were unimpressed with this tedious train, boat, and
balloon ride 'round the globe. The film that virtually invented the
"cameo," the costume drama-cum-travelogue extravaganza is a
must-see for movie buffs, who can test their mettle trying to spot the
forty-six bit parts of everyone from Marlene Dietrich and
Buster Keaton to Beatrice Lillie and Frank Sinatra.*

Albert Finney, Anthony Perkins, Vanessa Redgrave, Sean Connery, Ingrid Bergman, George Coulouris, Rachel Roberts, and Dame Wendy Hiller

MURDER ON THE ORIENT EXPRESS, 1974

One of the best-loved train flicks of all time by virtue of its outstanding all-star cast, this stylish tribute to Agatha Christie also starred a meticulously recreated facsimile of the world's most elegant train (the celebrated but long dormant Orient Express was relaunched not long after the film's premiere). Despite tepid reviews from critics, the film garnered a sympathy Oscar for Ingrid Bergman as Best Supporting Actress and spawned a spate of multi-star whodunit blockbusters, including Murder by Death, Death on the Nile, *and* The Mirror Crack'd.

Madeleine Carroll

THE GENERAL DIED AT DAWN, 1936

*Apparently filmed with the leftover sets from Paramount's
seminal railway classic,* Shanghai Express, *this Gary Cooper vehicle
again featured Eastern intrigue onboard a train chock-a-block with
Shanghai-bound shady characters. Billed with the hard-sell Hollywood
line, "Gary goes to town for the best-looking gal in China," this dry-as-
ice spin-off of the Josef von Sternberg/Marlene Dietrich classic
introduced American movie audiences to former London hat model
Carroll as the seductive spy who snares mercenary Cooper.*

Marlene Dietrich and Anna May Wong
SHANGHAI EXPRESS, 1932
*Winning a justly deserved Academy Award for its sumptuous
photography, this fourth collaborative effort from director Josef von
Sternberg and his muse, Marlene Dietrich, solidified their legend and
became the rule by which all future train pictures would be measured.
Introducing one of its star's signature characters ("It took more than one
man to change my name to Shanghai Lily"), the film transcends its
hooker-with-a-heart-of-gold theme to become a highly stylized montage
of stunning sets and deceptive characters, whose stop/go dialogue is
perfectly synchronized with the rhythm of the speeding train.*

**Margaret Lockwood, Michael Redgrave, Basil Radford,
Linden Travers, and Dame May Whitty**

THE LADY VANISHES, 1938

*Alfred Hitchcock's most brilliant British film and the one
that laid the tracks for his subsequent career in Hollywood, this
mystery/thriller/comedy mixes dazzling intrigue (an old lady suddenly
disappears on a train and only one person—Lockwood—seems to care)
with all the excitement you would hope to find on a luxury railroad car
speeding through Central Europe. So clever is the film's build-up
and high-speed denouement, that train buffs will even forgive the
preposterous model train used at the beginning of the picture.*

Claudette Colbert and Herbert Marshall
ZAZA, 1938 (ABOVE)

A remake of a David Belasco stage production that spawned two silent film versions (starring Pauline Frederick in 1915 and Gloria Swanson in 1923), this romantic trifle based on a popular French stage play about a can-can dancer who falls in love with a married aristocrat she meets on a train makes up in witty repartee what it lacks in originality. Demonstrating the kind of fast-and-frivolous drawing-room comedy she does best, French-born Colbert even sings a few tunes herself.

Claudette Colbert and Rudy Vallee
THE PALM BEACH STORY, 1942 (RIGHT)

Featuring the zaniest cast ever assembled in a screwball comedy, this Preston Sturges-directed gem about a wacky wife (Colbert) who runs away to catch a batty billionaire (Vallee) also features the most hilarious train sequence ever committed to celluloid. When the Ale and Quail Club hops aboard with stowaway Colbert, the ensuing ruckus leaves both the passengers of the Palm Beach-bound express and audiences everywhere howling in their seats.

Olivia deHavilland and Errol Flynn
DODGE CITY, 1939 (ABOVE)

*In the fifth of the nine collaborations between two of Hollywood's most
popular screen lovers, Flynn trades in his swashbuckling swords for a pair
of six-guns in order to clean up the wild west's great railway terminus
and sweeps deHavilland off her feet in the process. The inspiration for the
Mel Brooks spoof* Blazing Saddles, *this lusty Western boasts the big
screen's most ballyhooed barroom brawl and a blazing runaway train.*

Mae West and W. C. Fields
MY LITTLE CHICKADEE, 1940 (RIGHT)

*Although the pairing of two of Tinseltown's most popular comedic
actors would seem to have been an inspired idea, this shoot-'em-up spoof
of the wild west (written by the cantankerous duo) never really takes off,
although it features one of moviedom's most memorable train rides.
After picking off some marauding Indians from her train window, shady
Flower Belle Lee (West) trades insults and then marriage vows with
fellow passenger Cuthbert J. Twillie (Fields) in the most hilarious
celluloid wedding ceremony this side of the Chisolm Trail.*

Ingrid Bergman and Gregory Peck

SPELLBOUND, 1945

One of director Alfred Hitchcock's favorite cinematic settings, claustrophobic trains figure in many of the master's best-loved thrillers, including Strangers on a Train, The Lady Vanishes, *and this Oscar-winning entry about a repressed psychiatrist (Bergman) trying to unlock the even more repressed mind of her (possibly) psychopathic boss and would-be lover (Peck). Unbearably suspenseful per usual, the picture is derailed slightly by some pseudo-psychoanalytic mumbo jumbo and the jarring nightmare sequences furnished by none other than Salvador Dalí.*

Farley Granger and Robert Walker
STRANGERS ON A TRAIN, 1951
*Made at the height of Alfred Hitchcock's creative powers,
this over-analyzed masterpiece is also the director's most celebrated
train film. Remade in 1969 as* Once You Kiss a Stranger *and
the inspiration for the 1987 comedy hit* Throw Momma From
the Train, *the impeccably crafted tale of "exchange murders"
boasts Walker's penultimate and finest screen performance
(as the psychopath who carries out his end of the bargain)
and an explosive (literally) carousel climax.*

Lucille Ball and Bob Hope
FANCY PANTS, 1950 (ABOVE)
A remake of the 1935 comic smash Ruggles of Red Gap, *about a nouveau-riche wildcat who drags her English butler out west, this madcap musical update is most noteworthy for the inspired pairing of its two stars. Everyone's favorite professional coward, Hope is barely aboard the western-bound express before he runs into some shoot-'em-up trouble with a six-gun-slinging cowboy from the wrong side of the tracks.*

Moira Shearer and Anton Walbrook
THE RED SHOES, 1948 (RIGHT)
You don't have to be a balletomane to enjoy this magnificently photographed Oscar winner about a gorgeous redheaded dancer (Shearer) torn between her Diaghilev-like Svengali (Walbrook) and a young composer (Marius Goring). When a jealous Walbrook confronts his brilliant charge about her affections for the latter on a train bound for Monte Carlo, Shearer must decide between her career and love—with tragic consequences.

Renee Godfrey and Basil Rathbone
TERROR BY NIGHT, 1946 (ABOVE)
The Basil Rathbone/Nigel Bruce Sherlock Holmes mysteries were to run out of steam with this penultimate entry in the popular sleuth series. Featuring the obligatory eccentric passenger list and customary corpses, the train-format suspenser was made on a shoestring budget that manifested itself most glaringly in some comically inconsistent stock footage, including one too many engine changes en route from London to Edinburgh.

Margaret Lockwood, Rex Harrison, and Paul Henreid
NIGHT TRAIN TO MUNICH, 1940 (RIGHT)
Obviously inspired by the success of Alfred Hitchcock's The Lady Vanishes *(which also starred Lockwood), this high-speed comedy/spy thriller stands up to the Hitchcock original frame for frame in its action sequences, but lacks the master's light, witty touch. The tale of the double-crossed dealings between a Czech scientist's daughter (Lockwood), a British spy (Harrison), and a Gestapo agent (Henreid) during WWII, the film picks up steam during the terrifying final train sequence and hurtles to a spectacular cable-car climax.*

Marilyn Monroe, Jack Lemmon, and Tony Curtis
SOME LIKE IT HOT, 1959

*Only director Billy Wilder could elevate material of such obvious
bad taste (transvestism, impotence, slapstick, and crass one-liners)
into high art. A milestone in film comedy, this furiously-paced farce
about two musicians trying to elude the mob by posing as women
features the second-funniest Florida-bound train ride in film history.
(The Palm Beach Story gets the prize.) Sharing a berth with
ditzy-dame Monroe, Lemmon must put a lid on his lust and
settle for friendship in one memorable sleep-over scene.*

Eva Marie Saint and Cary Grant

NORTH BY NORTHWEST, 1959

A typically icy Hitchcock heroine, Saint loosens up enough to let Grant get the upper hand on the upper berth of a sleeping car in this classic tale of mistaken identity. More famous for its stars' climb down Mount Rushmore than this titillating train scene, the film is a compendium of much of the director's previous work, including The 39 Steps, Saboteur, *and* Foreign Correspondent.

Katharine Hepburn and Spencer Tracy

WITHOUT LOVE, 1945

Adapted from the Philip Barry play in which the outspoken, independent actress had starred on Broadway, Hepburn's third collaborative effort with Tracy had Hollywood's most discreet real-life lovers playing two people who marry for convenience and companionship—but not sex. Although the train scene in which the two must share a sleeping car is about as risqué as their pictures ever got, their nine films together made the beloved acting duo one of the most popular—and lucrative—celluloid couples of all time.

Sean Connery, Robert Shaw, and Daniela Bianchi
FROM RUSSIA WITH LOVE, 1963
The second James Bond flick features the world's most celebrated luxury locomotive (the Orient Express) as it wends its way from Istanbul to Venice. Adept as always at mixing business with pleasure, everyone's favorite secret agent manages to seduce one blonde spy (Bianchi) and fend off the other (Shaw, with an incredible dye job) in one of the most riveting railway rows in film history.

Carole Lombard and John Barrymore
TWENTIETH CENTURY, 1934

*Originally groomed as a standard-fare Hollywood glamour queen,
the actress "noted more for her slinky blonde looks, good legs, and
daring gowns than for anything else" became an overnight sensation
as a comedienne in this screwball farce directed by Howard Hawks and
featuring Barrymore in his last great role. The first comedy in which
sexy, sophisticated stars indulged in their own slapstick, this saucy
send-up of the theater world ends with a rip-roaring railway ride on
the Twentieth Century, as the two stars hurl insults, throw kisses, and
generally create havoc in one of the funniest films of the 1930s.*

Mary Carlisle, Una Merkel, Russell Hardie, and Charles Ruggles
MURDER IN THE PRIVATE CAR, 1934

Described by one critic at the time as "the swiftest 61 minutes of entertainment you are ever likely to see," this second-string MGM production is a kind of Murder on the Orient Express *without the pretense. Featuring a cast of some of Hollywood's most talented character actors, the film's expertly-staged climax between runaway railroad cars—as breathtaking and death-defying as any on film— proves that small budgets don't necessarily mean small pictures.*

Y. & W. R.I.

32

The Marx Brothers
Go West, 1940

While falling dismally short of the great train sequences in Buster Keaton's comedy classic, The General, *this late— and, thus, not great—Marx Brothers spoof of the wild west nevertheless has its moments. Tackling a vicious villain, the thr maniacs manage to save the day—if not the train!— in a crashing good climax that leaves passengers (and the aud ence) screaming with horror and laughter at the same time.*

Alexander Knox, Thomas Mitchell, and Geraldine Fitzgerald
WILSON, 1944 (ABOVE)
Raymond Massey
ABE LINCOLN IN ILLINOIS, 1940 (RIGHT)

Long before the era of airplanes, television, and FAX machines, presidents brought their messages to the people from the back platform of specially designed railway cars that traversed the nation from sea to shining sea. Two of the big screen's best-loved biopics featured award-winning portrayals of two of our best-loved leaders doing just that. Although President Wilson's post-WWI cross-country campaign to drum up support for the League of Nations cost him his health and, ultimately, support back in Washington, Lincoln fared better in his triumphant train-ride bid for election—a part that garnered Massey an Oscar nomination for the hit role he originated on Broadway.

Joel McCrea and Veronica Lake

SULLIVAN'S TRAVELS, 1941 (ABOVE)

Shamelessly publicized by Paramount with the line "There's no speed limit and no brake when Sullivan travels with Veronica Lake!", this Preston Sturges-directed tragicomedy about a movie director (McCrea) who becomes a hobo to get in touch with "reality" is less about the protagonist's escapades with his pint-sized, peekaboo-coiffed costar than it is a cleverly concealed tirade against Tinseltown. After meeting his future traveling companion in a hay-strewn boxcar, Sullivan thinks he has finally found "reality" traversing a Depression-blighted America, even as Hollywood soups up a publicity campaign about his adventures back home.

Harold Lloyd and Raymond Walburn

PROFESSOR, BEWARE! 1938 (RIGHT)

Still wearing his trademark black horn-rimmed glasses, the silent era's most successful comedian (he consistently out-earned his rivals Chaplin and Keaton) made only a few films after the advent of sound, including this cross-country romp from Paramount about a persnickety professor being pursued by art thieves aboard a speeding train. Performing his own stunt work into his mid-forties, the athletic Lloyd dangles from a rafter as a herd of steer crowds into a boxcar in one hilarious scene.

Paula Raymond and Ruby Dee

THE TALL TARGET, 1951 (ABOVE)

The unusual combination of period-piece drama and film-noir thriller
makes this Anthony Mann-directed suspenser a surprise treat.
The fictional story of a lone-wolf cop who believes an assassin lies in wait for
President Lincoln aboard a Baltimore-bound train, the inventively plotted
action comes to a head in the scene where Raymond and Dee watch a
man meet death under the wheels of the speeding locomotive.

Ernest Borgnine and Keith Carradine

EMPEROR OF THE NORTH POLE, 1973 (RIGHT)

Borgnine's boast that "no hobo has ever jumped my train and
lived to tell the tale" sets the tone for this Depression-era duel-to-the-death
actioner about a sadistic railwayman—armed with an awesome arsenal of
sledgehammers and steel chains—and the assorted bums who take him on.
Despite the film's joyless premise, scenes such as the thrilling train-top
game of brinkmanship between Borgnine and Carradine are
among the most harrowing action sequences of their kind.

Jon Voight
RUNAWAY TRAIN, 1985 (ABOVE)

The movie that Variety *magazine called "the most exciting epic
since* The Road Warrior*" is one of the most gripping runaway-train
stories of all time. Directed by Russian-born Andrei Konchalovsky, this
action-drenched drama about escaped convicts tearing across the tundra in
a hijacked train is as mean and cold as the Alaskan wasteland itself.
Two hours of unmitigated horror, the film finally climaxes with
a breakneck ride to the end of the line.*

James Dean
EAST OF EDEN, 1955 (LEFT)

*The story of Abel and Cain circa 1917, this Oscar-nominated
adaptation of the John Steinbeck novel was the first distinguished
production in CinemaScope and the precursor of the antihero films
that would proliferate in Hollywood over the next two decades. Although
Jo Van Fleet won an Academy Award for her riveting performance as the
quintessential hard-bitten harlot, it was rebel and icon-to-be Dean
(here hopping a ride to Nowhere) who emerged as an overnight
sensation in the first of his only three films.*

VON RYAN'S EXPRESS, 1965

This spectacular WWII thriller about a group of American
and British POWs who hijack a train climaxes on a slender viaduct
high in the Alps as the passengers fend off attacking Messerschmitts
while trying to unblock the tunnel that will take them to freedom.
About as realistic as a comic-book serial, the old-fashioned
adventure starring Frank Sinatra is just as much fun.

THE LADY VANISHES, 1979

*As noxious as the fumes spewing from this steam locomotive,
this much-publicized remake of the 1938 Alfred Hitchcock classic
retained the basic plot of the original but not the magic. Although
profiting somewhat from using real trains and location shooting,
the Cybill Shepherd-Elliott Gould vehicle was more a neatly packaged
showcase for the screwball antics of its superstar cast than a
fitting homage to the one-and-only master of suspense.*

"Broncho Billy" Anderson

THE GREAT TRAIN ROBBERY, 1903 (ABOVE)

*Not to be confused with the slick British flick by the same name made
three-quarters of a century later, the great-granddaddy of all train films
packed a lot of punch in its ten-minute running time (long, for those
days). The simple story of two bandits who tie up a telegraph operator and
rob a train, this Edison Studios release, the world's first Western and the
first picture to use technical tricks like the pan and the close-up,
made a star of its hero, who went on to make over 400
popular one-reelers during the next decade.*

SILENT SHORT, 1920s (RIGHT)

*Typical of many of the action-packed one-reelers that kept
matinee crowds glued to their seats, this silent-era short provided thrills
and laughs at the same time. Leaving more sophisticated humor for
Keaton and Lloyd, the unsung directors of these silver-screen fillers could
manipulate audience reaction by simply turning up the speed!*

SILVER STREAK, 1976 (LEFT)

An homage of sorts to the Alfred Hitchcock train-format susper[...]
this fake Thirties-style comedy/thriller about murder and mista[...]
identity aboard a Chicago-bound train features a few good mom[...]
especially when Gene Wilder engages in some Harold Lloyd-like [...]
work after he is thrown repeatedly from a moving railroad ca[...]
Despite a talented cast (Wilder, Jill Clayburgh, and Richard P[...]
and an exciting, if gratuitous, train-crash climax, the film [...]
lacks the finesse of Hitchcock's best work.

THE IRON HORSE, 1924 (PRECEDING PAGES)

<u>The</u> epic silent Western, this John Ford-directed classic
(his first important film) features a cast of thousands, authen[...]
steam locomotives, and the archetypal Western heroes who would [...]
a genre and take it to poetic heights. The story of the building of t[...]
transcontinental railway, the picture closes with the climactic mo[...]
when Manifest Destiny comes to an end as the two spurs of th[...]
railroad meet at Promontory Point, Utah, and join as one.

Peter O'Toole

LAWRENCE OF ARABIA, 1962

This David Lean-directed Best Picture Oscar-winner was made for the big screen. Shot on a 70-mm canvas, the stunningly photographed four-hour saga of the life and times of the Arab-loving English mercenary and would-be Messiah, T. E. Lawrence, features more frame-for-frame train explosions, derailments, murder, and mayhem than any other picture in film history (plus thirty-five minutes of recently released footage, if you haven't had enough).

**Charlton Heston, Cornel Wilde, James Stewart,
Betty Hutton, and Gloria Grahame**

THE GREATEST SHOW ON EARTH, 1952

*Train enthusiasts will love the big-time train-crash climax
of this Big Top extravaganza from director Cecil B. deMille. Boasting
an all-star cast second to none, the Paramount Studios salute to the
circus world brought the inventor of the big-budget Hollywood epic
his first Oscar after forty years in show business and featured a
talented supporting cast furnished by Ringling Brothers itself—
which was paid $250,000 for its name and services.*

Robert Walker, Alfred Hitchcock, and Farley Granger, 1951

*The master of suspense and the man who helped put
train movies on the Hollywood map poses for a publicity shot with
the stars of* Strangers on a Train, *one of his most famous. Although
Hitchcock never won an Academy Award, most of his fifty-seven
films—and scores of memorable train scenes—
have become silver-screen classics.*

CREDITS AND SOURCES

PROJECT EDITOR: J. C. SUARÈS
TEXT: J. SPENCER BECK
PICTURE EDITOR: LESLIE FRATKIN